Traverse Theatre Company

SWALLOW

by Stef Smith

First performed at the Traverse Theatre, Edinburgh,
on 9 August 2015

A Traverse Theatre Company Commission

SWALLOW

by Stef Smith

Company

Sam	Sharon Duncan-Brewster
Rebecca	Anita Vettesse
Anna	Emily Wachter

Director	Orla O'Loughlin
Designer	Fred Meller
Lighting Designer	Philip Gladwell
Composer/Sound Designer	Danny Krass
Assistant Director	Katherine Nesbitt
Additional Music	LAWholt
Voice	Ros Steen
Choreography	White & Givan

Production Manager	Kevin McCallum
Company Stage Manager	Gemma Turner
Deputy Stage Manager	Gary Morgan
Assistant Stage Manager	Jessica Ward
Costume Supervisor	Kat Smith

Foreword
from Director Orla O'Loughlin

It is February 2015. I am sitting in a packed studio theatre next to Traverse Executive Producer, Linda Crooks. Beside her is playwright Stef Smith. We are here, at the Doosan Arts Centre in Seoul, to see a public rehearsed reading of Stef's Traverse commission, *Swallow*. In Korean.

As ever at these kind of events, I watch the audience as much as the performance. I am very curious to know what these characters and their stories will mean here, over 5000 miles from home. I wonder how *Swallow* might translate narratively, emotionally, politically and culturally.

Linda, Stef and I share a giddy mix of jet lag and nerves before the performance starts, but once it does, we settle and, like the audience, are very focused and at times deeply moved. The play clearly takes flight with ease. The performers are very still and give enormously detailed and delicate performances. And the majority of the audience stay for a question-and-answer session following the show.

Questions for Stef relate mostly to her writing process, and for me are concerned with how I will direct the play. The audience have questions about how the play came into being and how, now it exists, it will translate into three dimensions. It strikes me very powerfully that no questions arise in relation to the characters, plot, themes or form. It seems that the world of *Swallow* is readily accepted in the terms within which it is presented.

I'm surprised and delighted. Surprised because *Swallow* isn't a straightforward kind of play. It is fragmentary, poetic and tonally diverse. It invites questions at every moment as to the who, what and why. I am thrilled that none of this gets in the way. Rather it creates an eloquence and internal logic all of its own.

The experience proves a shot in the arm for me. Proof, if it were needed, that *Swallow* is ready for production.

So, now, here I sit typing this. It is July 2015. I am in the Traverse rehearsal room in Leith. We are midway through week two and I am as inspired, challenged and excited as I have ever been about a project.

The actors and Stef are swapping romantic anecdotes in the green room, the gulls are squawking overhead and we are preparing to dive back in to the vivid, troubled and wonderful world of *Swallow*.

I'd like to thank the entire company for their fearless embrace of the play, its complications and celebrations. Dream creative and production teams for really going on the journey and supporting all our creative adventures. The actors for their bravery, tenacity and sheer class. And to Stef, for her tireless pursuit of better and for the blistering, clarion call of *Swallow*.

Foreword
from Writer Stef Smith

This process and play feel very special to me. I spent my student days seeing plays at the Traverse and, no matter where in the world I go, the Traverse will always be a particularly significant place for me, both professionally and personally. Over the last two years, I have had the utter privilege to work with some very generous and talented people who have supported me and spurred me on to write *Swallow*. The first draft of the play was written quickly and intensely, it just poured out onto the page. It was a play born of my absolute anger and anxiety that the world wasn't the place I felt it could be.

Creating this play has been a hard but hopeful process. Hard, because of the darkness it deals with – at times this play is raw and relentless – and ensuring a clarity in that can be a tough technical task. However, it has been hopeful because I've had the chance to share and swap stories with people who have made me feel a little less alone in my fears and fury. I hope too that I have helped them feel a little less alone.

Whether this play is a mirror to something you've felt or a window into an unfamiliar world, I hope that you see not particular answers to problems of the modern world, but rather you simply *see* the modern world. So often we see things how we wish to see them, because what is actually there is complex and contradictory with no solutions in sight. I often wonder whether we should call out these dark times rather than attempt to displace them. They might then have a little less control over us.

I've never doubted that we all wrestle with the chaos of deep, dark, hard things. We behave badly, drink too much, sleep too little, punch walls or pull our bodies apart. Rarely are we given the healthy tools that enable us to deal with this chaos. And yet, and yet, deal with it we do – we still get up the next day. And that's one of the main things that *Swallow* looks at – the chaotic ways in which we continue. After all, it's one of the things humanity does best. We continue or, at the very least, we try to.

So I'll let you continue on to the play. Enjoy, and good luck – with everything.

I'd like to say a special thanks to Orla O'Loughlin for her clarity, courage and creativity.

Biographies

SHARON DUNCAN-BREWSTER (SAM)
Previous theatre credits include *A Midsummer Night's Dream* (Liverpool Everyman); *Hope* (Royal Court); *The El Train* (Hoxton Hall); *Yerma* (Gate); *The Swan, There is a War* (National Theatre, London); *Tiger Country* (Hampstead); *Detaining Justice, Seize the Day, Category B, Let There Be Love, Fabulation, Playboy of the West Indies* (Tricycle); *The Horse Marines* (Theatre Royal Plymouth); *The Bacchae* (National Theatre of Scotland); *Black Crows* (Clean Break/Arcola); *Magic Carpet* (Lyric Hammersmith); *Blues For Mr Charlie* (Tricycle/New Wolsey); *Dirty Butterfly* (Soho); *Peepshow* (Frantic Assembly/Plymouth/Lyric); *Keepers* (Hampstead); *Crave* (Paines Plough); *So Special* (Manchester Royal Exchange); *Yard Gal* (Clean Break/Royal Court); *The No Boys Cricket Club* (Stratford East Theatre Royal) and *Babies* (Royal Court). Television credits include *Unforgotten, Cuffs, Cucumber, The Mimic, The Bible, Top Boy, Holby City, Casualty, Doctor Who, EastEnders, Doctors, Shoot the Messenger, Waking the Dead, Baby Father, Hope I Die Before I Get, Bad Girls, Body Story*, and *The Bill*. Film credits include *Three and Out* (Rovinge); *The Child* (Rider's to the Sea Ltd) and *Blues for Nia*.

PHILIP GLADWELL (LIGHTING DESIGNER)
Previous work for the Traverse includes Fringe First Award-winning *Ciara, I'm With the Band, The Arthur Conan Doyle Appreciation Society, In the Bag* and *Melody*. Other theatre credits include *The James Plays* (National Theatre of Scotland & National Theatre); *The World of Extreme Happiness, Love the Sinner* (National Theatre); *The Twits, Liberian Girl, The Ritual Slaughter of Gorge Mastromas, No Quarter, Oxford Street, Kebab* (Royal Court); *Mr Burns, Before the Party* (Almeida); *Miss Julie* (Schaubühne, Berlin); *LIMBO* (Nominated for the WhatsOnStage Best Lighting Design); *A Midsummer Night's Dream* (Barbican/US tour); *Further than the Furthest Thing* (Dundee Rep, winner CATS Best Design); *Amazonia, Ghosts, The Member of the Wedding, Festa!* (Young Vic); *The King & I, Happy Days – A New Musical, Radio Times* (UK tour); *One for the Road, God of Carnage, The Festival of Chaos, Two Gentlemen of Verona, The Duchess of Malfi* (Royal & Derngate, Northampton); *Small Hours* (Hampstead); *Five Guys Named Moe* (Underbelly/Theatre Royal Stratford East); *Terminus* (Abbey Dublin/Australia/New York/Young Vic; Fringe First Edinburgh); *Cinderella, Aladdin* (Lyric Hammersmith); *Mogadishu, Punk Rock* (Lyric Hammersmith/UK tour); *Too Clever by Half, You Can't Take It With You, Nineteen Eighty-Four, Macbeth* (Manchester Royal Exchange); *My Romantic History* (Bush/Sheffield; Fringe First Edinburgh); *The Fahrenheit Twins, Low Pay? Don't Pay!* (Told by an Idiot); *Obama the Mamba, Gypsy, Chicago, The Sound of Music* (Curve); *For Once* (Pentabus); *Once on This Island* (Hackney Empire); *Harvest* (UK tour); *Testing the Echo* (Out of Joint); *The Spire, Design for Living,*

Drowning on Dry Land (Salisbury Playhouse); *Pastoral, The Boy Who Fell into a Book, Overspill, HOTBOI* (Soho). Opera and ballet credits include *Rigoletto* and *La Wally* (Opera Holland Park); *After Dido* (ENO); *Così fan tutte* (WNO); *Awakening* and *Another America: Fire* (Sadler's Wells); *Il Tabarro, Suor Angelica* and *Gianni Schicchi* (Opera Zuid); *Falstaff* (Grange Park Opera) and the concert performances of Stravinsky's Violin Concerto, George Benjamin's Dance Figures, Bartok's Concerto for Orchestra and Stravinsky's *Oedipus Rex* (Royal Festival Hall).

DANNY KRASS (COMPOSER/SOUND DESIGNER)
Danny's previous work for the Traverse includes *The Artist Man and The Mother Woman, Quiz Show, Spoiling* and *The Devil Masters*. Other theatre credits include *Who Cares* (Royal Court); *Magic Sho, The Curious Scrapbook of Josephine Bean, Huff* (Shona Reppe Puppets); *Smokies* (Solar Bear); *The Voice Thief, Stuck, The Ballad of Pondlife McGurk, White, Kes* (Catherine Wheels); *Up to Speed* (Imaginate/ Ros Sydney); *The Adventures of Robin Hood* (Visible Fictions/Kennedy Centre); *My House, A Small Story* (Starcatchers); *Peter Pan* (Sherman Cymru); *Skewered Snails, He-La* (Iron Oxide); *Mikey and Addie, Littlest Christmas Tree, Rudolf, Mr Snow, The Little Boy that Santa Claus Forgot* (Macrobert); *The Infamous Brothers Davenport* (Vox Motus/ Royal Lyceum, Edinburgh); *One Thousand Paper Cranes* (Lu Kemp); *The Day I Swapped My Dad for Two Goldfish, The Tin Forest* (National Theatre of Scotland); *Couldn't Care Less* (Plutôt la Vie/Strange Theatre); *Sanitise* (Melanie Jordan and Caitlin Skinner); *Eat Me* (A Moment's Peace); and *Waves* (Alice Cooper). Upcoming projects include *International Waters* (Fire Exit); *My Friend Selma* (Terra Incognita) and *Kind of Silence*, a sound-led piece for Solar Bear Theatre which will be Danny's directorial debut.

LAWholt (ADDITIONAL MUSIC)
Rising star LAWholt is an Edinburgh-based singer-songwriter. She performs with a distinctively primal vocal style set against experimental electronic music from producer Tim London. Recently appearing on BBC *Introducing*, she is a regular collaborator with Mercury Prize-winning hip-hop trio, Young Fathers. Her debut EP *Haters and Gangsters* was released in 2014. www.lawholt.com

FRED MELLER (DESIGNER)
Fred is a freelance international scenographer and theatre designer. She trained at the Royal Welsh College and received an Arts Council Designers Bursary. She has designed for the Royal Shakespeare Company, Cardboard Citizens, the Almeida, Gate Theatre, Royal National Theatre Studio, Watermill Theatre, Nuffield Theatre, Royal Court Theatre, the Young Vic, Kaos and Grid Iron. Fred often works in new writing and in non-theatre spaces such as an old hospital, jam factory, a mortuary, a disused brothel, Victorian labyrinthine Town Hall cellars, a supermarket

distribution complex, and the biggest potting shed in Europe. She has also created a broad and diverse range of work for traditional theatre buildings. Fred exhibited at the Prague Quadrennial in 1999 and 2003, winning the Golden Triga and was selected to exhibit at the World Stage Design in Toronto 2005, and in the National Society of British Theatre Designers exhibitions. Her work is part of the V&A Museum permanent collection. Other awards include The Jerwood Design Award and a Year of the Artist Award. She is course leader for the BA (Hons) Performance Design and Practice course at Central Saint Martins, University of the Arts, London. She is a Co-convenor of the scenography working group at TaPRA (Theatre and Performance Research Association), a Fellow of the HEA, and a Fellow of The Arts Foundation.

KATHERINE NESBITT (ASSISTANT DIRECTOR)
This is Katherine's first role with the Traverse Theatre. She is Artistic Director of Makeshift Broadcast, based in Glasgow. She was a recipient of a Federation of Scottish Theatre Assistant Director Bursary in 2013–14. Her work as assistant director includes *A Walk at the Edge of the World*, *Rough Mix* (Magnetic North); *My Glasgow* (Terra Incognita/Scottish Refugee Council) and *Little Red Riding Hood* (The Arches). Her work as a director includes *When the Rain Stops Falling* (Tron); *Putting Words in My Mouth* (The Arches/Prague Fringe); *Bike* (Buzzcut); *Ice Nine* (CCA Glasgow); *(Un)Known Unknowns* (New Works New Worlds Festival); *The Company of Wolves* (The Arches/Forest Fringe); *Attempts on Her Life* (West End Festival) and *Dr. Faustus* (Gilmorehill Theatre). Katherine is supported in this role by the JMK Trust and is a Leverhulme Arts Scholar.

ORLA O'LOUGHLIN (DIRECTOR)
Orla is Artistic Director of the Traverse Theatre. Prior to taking up post at the Traverse, she was Artistic Director of the award-winning Pentabus Theatre and International Associate at the Royal Court Theatre. Orla has also received the JMK Award and Carlton Bursary at the Donmar Warehouse. Directing work for the Traverse includes the Scotsman Fringe First Award-winning *Spoiling*, the Scotsman Fringe First, Herald Angel and CATS Award-winning *Ciara*, *The Devil Masters*, *Clean*, *A Respectable Widow Takes to Vulgarity*, *Fifty Plays for Edinburgh*, *The Arthur Conan Doyle Appreciation Society*, *The Artist Man and the Mother Woman,* and the Herald Angel Award-winning *Dream Plays* (Scenes From a Play I'll Never Write). Other directing work includes *For Once* (Hampstead Theatre Studio/UK tour); *Kebab* (Dublin International Festival/Royal Court); *How Much Is Your Iron?* (Young Vic); *The Hound of the Baskervilles* (West Yorkshire Playhouse/UK tour/West End); *Tales of the Country*, *Origins* (Pleasance/Theatre Severn); *Relatively Speaking, Blithe Spirit, Black Comedy* (Watermill); *Small Talk: Big Picture* (BBC World Service/ICA/Royal Court); *A Dulditch Angel* (UK tour) and *The Fire Raisers, sob stories, Refrain* (BAC).

STEF SMITH (PLAYWRIGHT)

Stef Smith studied Drama and Theatre Arts at Queen Margaret University in Edinburgh. Stef wrote the text for the critically acclaimed play *RoadKill* (Edinburgh Festival 2010, 2011). The show won a number of awards including a Fringe First, a Herald Angel and the Amnesty International Freedom of Expression Award. In 2012, *RoadKill* transferred to Theatre Royal Stratford East and subsequently won the Olivier Award for Outstanding Achievement in an Affiliate Theatre and then toured to Paris, Chicago and New York. Other credits include *Remote* (NT Connections, nationwide); *And the Beat Goes On* (Random Accomplice and Perth Horsecross Theatre, Scottish tour); *CURED* (Glasgay!); *Smoke (and Mirrors)* (Theatre Uncut); *Woman of the Year* (Òran Mór); *Grey Matter* (Lemon Tree, Aberdeen); *The Silence of Bees, Falling/Flying* (Tron, Glasgow) and *Tea and Symmetry* (BBC Radio Scotland). Stef has also been on attachment with the National Theatre of Scotland, an invited residency at the Banff Centre in Canada and is currently under commission at the Royal Court Theatre.

ANITA VETTESSE (REBECCA)

Anita trained at the Royal Conservatoire of Scotland, Glasgow. Previous theatre credits include *In Time of Strife, Men Should Weep, Macbeth, The Wolves in the Walls* (National Theatre of Scotland); *The War Hasn't Started Yet, Perfect Stroke* (Òran Mór); *Beowulf, Talk To Me Like the Rain, Suddenly Last Summer, Monaciello* (Tron/Napoli Teatro Festivali); *Blithe Spirit, Sabina, Educating Rita* (Perth Theatre); *Fleeto/Wee Andy* (Tumult In The Clouds); *The Infamous Brothers Davenport* (Vox Motus/Lyceum); *Slab Boys, Cat on a Hot Tin Roof, While the Sun Shines* (The Byre Theatre); *Freefall, Private Agenda, Can't Pay Won't Pay* (7:84); *Accidental Death of an Anarchist, Chooky Brae* (Borderline); *Smalltown* (Random Accomplice); *West Side Story/Romeo and Juliet* (Courtyard Theatre, Hereford); *Last One Out* (Scottish Opera). Anita's television credits include *Shetland, Hollyoaks, Bob Servant, The Crash, Waterloo Road, Poe's Women, Single Father, Taggart, River City, The Angry Brigade, The Bill, The Bill Bailey Show*. Her film credits include *Tuesday, Tide, The Legend of Barney Thompson, Hector, Birthday* and *The Road Above,* whilst her radio work includes *Tender is the Night, The Sensitive, Going Spare, 44 Scotland Street, Boxer and Doberman and Baby's Coming Back* (all for BBC Radio). Anita is also writing her first play for Òran Mór, for the autumn season 2015, touring to the Sherman Cymru in Cardiff and the Tobacco Factory in Bristol.

EMILY WACHTER (ANNA)

Emily trained at Rose Bruford College and at École Internationale de Théâtre Jacques LeCoq, Paris. Previous theatre credits include *From Morning to Midnight* (National Theatre, London); *Julius Caesar* (Royal Shakespeare Company); *Caucasian Chalk Circle, Britain's Best Recruiting Sergeant* (Unicorn); *Bedroom Farce, Separate Tables* (Salisbury Playhouse); *The Humans* (Avignon Festival); *Rats' Tales* (Manchester Royal Exchange); *The Master Builder* (Chichester Festival Theatre); *Pride and Prejudice* (Theatre Royal Bath); *Origins* (Edinburgh Festival/Pentabus); *Blithe Spirit* (Watermill) and *A Midsummer Night's Dream* (Ludlow Festival). Television credits include *Psychoville, Compulsion, Judge John Deed* and *Booze Cruise*. Radio credits include *Northanger Abbey, The Tales of King Arthur, The Way We Live Right Now, Claire in the Community* and *High Table, Low Orders*. Emily has also received the Carleton Hobbs Radio Award.

WHITE & GIVAN (CHOREOGRAPHY)

As performers and choreographers with over twenty-five years of experience, White & Givan Co-Artistic Directors Errol White and Davina Givan have a wealth of experience they have fed into the company since its inception in 2009 under the former name, Errol White Company. They have both performed internationally for many years, working alongside such distinguished directors and choreographers as Rui Horta, Darshan Singh Buller, Richard Alston, Wayne McGregor, Bob Cohan, and Janet Smith among many others. In addition to their extensive performing and repertory work they are respected and valued education practitioners, having spent four years as Artistic and Creative Directors of National Youth Dance Wales, and have taught extensively across the UK. Since 2009 the company has received generous support from Creative Scotland, which has allowed Errol and Davina to share their artistic work and practitioner experience with the Scottish dance community. They've staged three successful and critically acclaimed Scottish tours of company work (*Three Works*, 2009, *IAM*, 2012 & *Breathe*, 2014) and in 2014 they successfully launched and ran a pilot of Evolve, Scotland's first paid dance apprenticeship for dancers.

ROS STEEN (VOICE)

Ros has worked extensively in theatre, film and television. Work for the Traverse includes *Ciara, The Artist Man and The Mother Woman, The Goat or Who is Sylvia?, The Last Witch* (Traverse/Edinburgh International Festival); *Damascus, Carthage Must Be Destroyed, strangers babies, Tilt, Shimmer, Dark Earth, Homers, Outlying Islands, Heritage, Solemn Mass for a Full Moon in Summer* (as co-director); *Knives in Hens, Passing Places*. Other recent work includes *Macbeth, Let the Right One In, Glasgow Girls, Black Watch* (National Theatre of Scotland); *Cyrano de*

Bergerac (Northern Stage/Royal & Derngate); *Fever Dream Southside, True West* (Citizens' Theatre); *Hedda Gabler, Bondagers, The Lieutenant of Inishmore, Mary Queen of Scots Got Her Head Chopped Off* (Royal Lyceum); *Blood Wedding* (Dundee Rep/Graeae/Derby Playhouse); *Great Expectations, The Glass Menagerie, In My Father's Words* (Dundee Rep); *A Walk at the Edge of the World, Sex and God, Walden* (Magnetic North). Television and film credits include *God Help the Girl, I Love Luci, Hamish Macbeth, Monarch of the Glen* and *2,000 Acres of Sky*. Radio credits include *Cloud Howe, The Other One, Gondwanaland* (BBC Radio 4). Ros is an Emeritus Professor at the Royal Conservatoire of Scotland.

Traverse Theatre Company

'One of the most exciting places for theatre in the UK.'
Guardian

The Traverse is Scotland's foremost theatre company dedicated to new writing.

Founded by a group of passionate arts enthusiasts seeking to extend the spirit of the Festival throughout the year, the Traverse Theatre Club opened in a former brothel in Edinburgh's Lawnmarket in 1963. Now, more than a half-century on, the Traverse is an established part of Scotland's arts infrastructure, yet retains that essence of innovation and excitement. It remains committed to the original spirit of its founders, and to presenting audiences with a good story, well told. Under Artistic Director Orla O'Loughlin it continues to produce vibrant theatre for, and of, our time, further building its reputation with award-winning productions such as *The Artist Man and The Mother Woman*, *Quiz Show*, *Ciara* and *Spoiling*.

Internationally acclaimed as a powerhouse of new writing, the Traverse has launched the careers of some of Scotland's most celebrated writers, including John Byrne, David Greig, Gregory Burke, David Harrower, Liz Lochhead and Zinnie Harris. Many of today's finest actors have appeared on its stages, including Tilda Swinton, Billy Connolly, Robbie Coltrane, Bill Nighy and Alan Cumming.

The Traverse's impact is truly international: it frequently tours overseas, engages in artistic exchanges and partnerships – most recently in Québec, Turkey and South Korea – and, every August, it holds an iconic status as the theatrical heart of the Edinburgh Festival Fringe.

Always looking to the future, the Traverse leads Participation and Engagement programmes that engage with emerging writers and artistic talent to develop the next generation of theatre-makers.

Special Thanks

The work of the Traverse Theatre would not be possible without the support of:

ALBA | CHRUTHACHAIL

The Traverse extends grateful thanks to the many individuals, organisations, trusts and foundations that support and contribute to the theatre's work. Each plays an important part in securing the Traverse's future and maintaining its reputation as one of the world's most exciting theatres.

With special thanks to Alan & Penny Barr, Katie Bradford, Iain Millar and Bridget Stevens.

Traverse Productions are generously supported by Cotterell & Co and Paterson SA Hairdressing.

Special thanks for *Swallow* go to: National Theatre Studios; Royal Lyceum Theatre Company; Doosan Arts Centre; CJ, Jamie Pallas and Dr Catherine McNamara at Gendered Intelligence; Colin Oulton; Jo Elliott, Rachel Goddard, Chris West and Barbara Smith at The Royal Zoological Society of Scotland (RZSS Edinburgh Zoo); Gerry and all at Unsub Actors; Jo Clifford; Aisling McBride; Dr Ashley Miller; Nicola Jo Cully; Kate Dickie; Meg Fraser; Mary Gapinski; Sarah McCardie; Kirsty McKay; Adura Onashile; Francis Thorburn; Gail Watson; Arran & Alex; Catherine Grosvenor; Zinnie Harris; Hamish Pirie; Mhari and Glenn Robinson; Gilly Roche; Rose Ruane; Davina Shah; Suzanne Smith; and all those who helped in the research and development of *Swallow*.

Connect with us

TravCast

Find our monthly podcasts on **soundcloud.com** and **traverse.co.uk** with insights into the making of shows and featuring interviews with some of the UK's leading writers.

Traverse Theatre

The Company

Fiona Campbell	Box Office Manager
Jessica Chalmers	Box Office Senior Supervisor
Linda Crooks	Executive Producer & Joint Chief Executive
Claire Doohan	Marketing & Campaigns Officer
Claire Elliot	Deputy Electrician
Kisha Gallagher	Trading Company Manager
Ellen Gledhill	Development Manager
Tom Grayson	Deputy Box Office Manager
Rose Gregory	Trading Company Assistant Manager
Zinnie Harris	Associate Director
Rosie Kellagher	Literary Associate
Jonathan Kennedy	Technical Theatre Apprentice
Rebecca Leary	Receptionist/Administrator
Kath Lowe	Front of House Manager
Catherine Makin	Artistic Administrator
Francisca Martinez Garcia	Senior Kitchen Supervisor
Kevin McCallum	Head of Production
Bradley McCathie	Traverse Trading Senior Supervisor
Ruth McEwan	Assistant Producer
Ann Monfries	Head of Marketing & Sales
Ondine Oberlin	Box Office Supervisor
Orla O'Loughlin	Artistic Director & Joint Chief Executive
Cian O'Siochain	Press and Media Officer
Joy Parkinson	Marketing & Communications Assistant
Julie Pigott	Head of Finance & Administration
David Pollock	Operations Manager
Pauleen Rafferty	Payroll & HR Manager
Sunniva Ramsay	Engagement Co-ordinator
Renny Robertson	Chief Electrician
Michelle Sandham	Finance Officer
Tom Saunders	Lighting & Sound Technician
Gary Staerck	Head of Stage

Also working for the Traverse

Eleanor Agnew, Charlotte Anderson, Lindsay Anderson, Calum Brittain, Emma Campbell, Ben Clifford, Amy Cloonan, Hannah Cornish, Rachel Cullen, Koralia Daskalaki, Jonathan Dawson, Caitlin Delves, Euan Dickson, Judith Dobie, Uxia Dominguez Rial, Christine Dove, Rachel Duke, Calum Dwyer, Katherine Eggleston, Sarah Farrell, Daniel Findlay-Carroll, Sorcha Fitzgerald, Andrew Gannon, Anthony Gowling, Laura Grantham, Megan Hampton, Charles Hanks, Laura Hawkins, David Howie, Jennifer Hulse, Adam James, Miguel Leonisio Torrejon, Lynsey MacKenzie, Alan Massie, Cristina Matthews, Cleo McCabe, Kieran McCruden, Kirsty McIntyre, Edwin Milne, Alasdair Mitchell, Stephen Moir, Hal Morrissey Gillman, Liam Pike, Anna Reid, Simon Rutherford, Theodora Sakellaridou, Kolbrun Sigfusdottir, Rosalind Sim, Kathryn Smith, Olivia Stoddart, Joanne Sykes, Emma Taylor, Hannah Ustun, Jessica Ward, Rosemary Ward

Associate Artists

Emma Callander	Associate Artist
Clare Duffy	IASH/Traverse Creative Fellow
David Greig	Associate Artist
Morna Pearson	Associate Artist
Tim Price	Associate Artist
Ellie Stewart	BBC Writersroom 10 Writer
Stef Smith	Associate Artist

Traverse Theatre Board of Directors

Sir John Elvidge (Chair)
Adrienne Sinclair Chalmers (Company Secretary)
Barbara Allison
Roy McEwan
Adrian O'Donnell
Christopher Wyn

SWALLOW

Stef Smith

'I used to think I was the strangest person in the world but then I thought there are so many people in the world, there must be someone just like me who feels bizarre and flawed in the same ways I do. I would imagine her, and imagine that she must be out there thinking of me too. Well, I hope that if you are out there and read this and know that, yes, it's true I'm here, and I'm just as strange as you.'

Frida Kahlo
As quoted in *Vogue*, 1937

Characters

REBECCA
SAM
ANNA

All the characters are in their thirties or forties. They can be any race, the reference to Sammy Davis Jr. on page 5 should be changed according to the race of the performer playing Sam.

A (/) at the end of a sentence denotes an interrupted line.

There are no stage directions, imagine it as you wish.

This text went to press before the end of rehearsals and so may differ slightly from the play as performed.

ANNA   Who said smashing things up was a bad thing? It's actually quite liberating. People should really smash up more things. Sweat drips down my back as I stand in the middle of my living room clutching a claw hammer. I should have done this sooner, after all – they're just *things*.

REBECCA My lipstick clings to the rim of the glass. I meant to have just one glass while I waited but – half the bottle is gone. I think about being back in his arms. I think about how long it's been since his beard brushed against my cheek. I think about... fuck, I should have shaved my legs.

SAM   I draw the curtains, and I take the cigarette out my pocket. I've been practising holding it for days, trying to make it look natural, trying to make it look like it's part of me. I place the cigarette in my mouth. The taste of tar already touches my tongue and I take a match out of the box. I run it along the side and that sulphur smell fills the air. Rich and raw.

REBECCA I just want him back.

ANNA   God bless hammers.

SAM   Light.

REBECCA I just want him home.

SAM   Inhale.

ANNA   I raise it above the mirror and shout /

ALL   / Fuck this.

SAM   I don't smoke. But here I am trying to swallow the smoke of this fag as I stand lingering in the mirror. I've got a PhD in picking myself apart and I was stupid to think I'd see someone more like Sammy Davis Jr. and less like me.

ANNA   I hit it again. Another crack. I hit it again and it
              splinters. The shards are all over the floor and it's
              just beautiful because that was the last one – the
              last mirror in my flat. I've been waiting for this.
              Keeping this moment safe.

REBECCA   Warm white wine and mirrors everywhere. Some
              1980s nonsense is being played too loud. He
              always had a terrible taste in restaurants and it still
              makes me smile.

SAM   Smoke.

ANNA   Splinter.

REBECCA   Soave.

ANNA   After I stopped going out, I needed to pace my
              projects. It's been nearly two Christmases since I
              last stepped out of my front door, and it's really
              given me the focus I needed.

REBECCA   I look at that woman. That woman in the mirror
              who is me, she is always older than I remember.
              And out the corner of my eye.

ANNA   Vitamin D is overrated.

REBECCA   I see him.

SAM   I stole this cigarette from work.

ANNA   Fresh air is overrated.

REBECCA   My thighs clench.

SAM   I didn't want to pay for twenty of them if this
              wasn't something I was going to truly commit to.

REBECCA   We hug and it hurts that his clothes no longer
              smell like mine.

ANNA   Who needs out there when I'm so busy in here.

REBECCA   I use my fingers under the table to count how
              many months it's been since I last saw him.
              Five months and half a thumb.

SAM   Standing, smoking and choking. Trying.

ANNA   With this smashed mirror and some feathers I
            found on my windowsill and an old jar of pesto I
            found in the back of my fridge – I will make a
            mosaic. I haven't eaten solids in weeks so the
            pesto was only going to go to waste – after all,
            tasting and chewing are overrated. I used to worry
            that I had gone mad but really I have no time for
            that. Going crazy is a full-time job and I've got
            things to do. Things that need doing.

SAM   I take one pair of balled-up sports socks and stuff
            them down my jeans. I feel the bulge. I cup it. I
            hold it. I push it forward. A burning in my
            stomach. Fire and flames.

REBECCA   You've met someone else?

            But you were… we were…

            I stand up and bang my head on this low-hanging
            lamp. Some reclaimed shit.

            I throw my ring at him. Across the table. He
            catches it in the folds of his shirt.

            The whole restaurant is looking at me, so I pick up
            my Primark bag, inhale my glass of wine and run.

ANNA   When I look into my mosaic I see only parts of
            me. Moments of me. And those feathers. Those
            beautiful feathers.

            I switch the TV on.

            It's just me and the shards and the TV screen now.
            Everyone else has given up on me. And it's my
            favourite TV programme. I like programmes about
            places I'll never go.

SAM   I pull out a black felt-tip pen. Snap the cap off. The
            smell of the ink hits my nose. I lift the pen to my
            face. I begin to do the outline. The shape of a beard.

REBECCA   Back at my house. I storm through the front door.
            Open a cupboard in the kitchen and pull out a half
            bottle of… Midori? I fill the glass all the way up

to the top. Then I just throw the whole glass at the wall.

I throw the bottle at the wall.

I throw another glass.

SAM   I draw on my cheeks, on my chin.

ANNA   This one's my favourite.

REBECCA   I throw another.

SAM   Thicker and harder.

ANNA   And I like this one.

REBECCA   Another

SAM   And again

ANNA   This one

REBECCA   Another

SAM   Again

ANNA   This one

REBECCA   Another

SAM   Again

ANNA   This one

REBECCA   Another

SAM   Again

ANNA   This one

REBECCA   Another

SAM   Again

REBECCA   Stop.

Silence.

SAM   I look. I look.

ANNA   I stare into that screen.

SAM   I just.

REBECCA   Pull out my phone, begin to write one new
            message.

SAM   I smudge the ink across my face onto my hands.

ANNA   I press my hands onto the glass.

SAM   I just wanted to see.

REBECCA   I send him one word – ASSHOLE.

            I send it to him twenty-three times. Asshole.
            Asshole. Asshole. Asshole. Asshole. Asshole.
            Asshole. Asshole. Asshole. Asshole. Asshole.
            Asshole. Asshole. Asshole. Asshole. Asshole.
            Asshole. Asshole. Asshole. Asshole. Asshole.
            Asshole. Asshole. (*Lines run under the following
            text*.)

SAM   I hold myself higher.

ANNA   Eyeballs scraping that screen.

SAM   Solider. Stronger.

ANNA   This episode is about birds of the rainforest.

SAM   From here on in my name is Sam.

ANNA   Fly above it. Above it all.

REBECCA   I stumble into my kitchen. Forgetting about the
            mound of broken glass and glittering fuck-uppery.
            And before I know it I put my foot down and I slip.

SAM   No going back.

REBECCA   I hit the ground. I land face-first into a pile of glass.

ANNA   Fragments of something.

REBECCA   Shock covers my skin.

ANNA   Pieces placed so precisely.

SAM   Forwards now.

REBECCA   I sit up.

            I feel the warm trickle of blood down my cheek.
            It's been pierced with a piece of glass. Right the
            way through all that muscle. A piece almost as big

as a playing card. My tongue gently skates across it. And just before I go to pull it out. I push it. I let it tear into my skin a bit more. I want to feel it. Like really feel it. Blood pours into my mouth, I taste iron, I swallow it. I get this rush of pain. This rush of delight. No logic. No emotions. Just

SAM   Flame

ANNA   Fragments

REBECCA   Free.

Silence.

It took twelve little thread in-and-outs to close that hole in my cheek. The doctor said I overreacted. I told him to go fuck himself.

I promised myself I would leave the house today. To try and get back in the world. With this... new face. But people stare. People wonder what happened. They whisper, they point. They think I can't hear. Freak. Frankenstein /

SAM   / Is anyone sitting here?

Silence.

All the other seats are taken. I'm just doing the gentlemanly thing /

REBECCA   / No.

SAM   Just want to drink my coffee.

REBECCA   Go ahead.

SAM   Was it a good one?

REBECCA   What?

SAM   Daydream.

REBECCA   Nothing special.

SAM   That's a shame.

ANNA   Sixteen cuts on my fingers but my mosaic is complete. It's garlic and feathers... it's beautiful.

The way the light... the way it just... Yes... This is exactly how I imagined it.

SAM   You shouldn't waste a daydream.

REBECCA   Oh... right.

SAM   She rolls her eyes.

REBECCA   I've got a busy head.

SAM   Picks off her nail polish.

REBECCA   Hard to daydream properly when... never mind.

SAM   She looks at me, without a blink.

REBECCA   He does this warm smile and I can't think of anything to smile about.

ANNA   It's always such a pity when a project ends. It's always so... so terribly... I have to be careful with too much stillness.

SAM   Was it an accident? Your. Sorry I didn't mean to /

REBECCA   / A car crash. It was a car crash. I'm lucky to be alive.

             That's what I'm meant to say, isn't it?

SAM   You can say what you want. I don't know you.

ANNA   Before my mosaic I made these little bird feeders. I covered all my tampons with honey and granola and hung them off the handle of the window. The pigeons landed one by one. I once saw one of them eat a whole tampon and thirty seconds later the pigeon just exploded. Feathers everywhere – must have been one of those extra-absorbent ones.

SAM   I'm Sam.

REBECCA   Good for you.

ANNA   Now it's time for something new.

             Something bigger.

SAM   Because this is the first time I /

REBECCA   / It's nice to meet you, *Sam*.

SAM   Nice to meet you…

REBECCA   Rebecca.

ANNA   Something unlike anything that came before.

SAM   Rebecca.

ANNA   I stand on a chair in the living room to watch the birds make nests in the roof across the road. I watch them build for hours – it's just exquisite.

REBECCA   I decide to take them out, I'll take the stitches out myself. Nail scissors under the thread. Snip, snip, snip. Done. A face with the flash of a pink line. Scarred.

SAM   My father always used to say there is nothing gaffer tape won't fix. So I place it just under my armpit. I begin to wrap the tape around my chest. And I slowly see, the black shine of the tape pressing my chest flat. It's like part of me has been deleted. Perfect.

ANNA   I find the hammer, two drawers left of the cooker. I unplug my phone and just slam that hammer down onto it. I never liked having a phone anyway. Too much anticipation. A woman at my old work used to masturbate with her mobile. She got it stuck up there once during her lunch break. She called herself from a pay phone to see if it was on. She took the rest of the day off after that… But these little parts of the telephone. Well, they'll be just perfect for my next idea.

REBECCA   I go to play with my wedding ring, and every time I get a little spike of shock when it's not there. But I've got to be… I must remind myself there is /

SAM   / You got your stitches out?

     It's Sam /

REBECCA   / I know.

SAM   Have you had a nice week?

REBECCA   Uneventful.

SAM   Is that a good or a bad thing?

REBECCA   Are you just going to stand /

SAM   / Can I /

REBECCA   / Do what you like.

SAM   Are you on your lunch break?

REBECCA   No… Are you?

SAM   I work nights.

REBECCA   Why?

SAM   I work at a residential unit.

REBECCA   I couldn't do that. Too hard. Too sad.

SAM   What is it you /

REBECCA   / Paralegal. I'm taking some time away from work. Can't greet clients with a face like this.

SAM   Well, I think your face is just fine.

REBECCA   And I think you're a good liar. I'm not having a very good day, week, year. Let's call it a run of very bad luck.

SAM   I don't believe in luck.

REBECCA   What do you believe in?

SAM   I don't know. Do you smoke?

Silence.

We don't have to talk, we could just /

REBECCA   / Fine.

SAM   Fine.

ANNA   My favourite blouse. Silk. White. Almost translucent if you hold it to the light. Beautiful. So I take a pair of scissors and I slice right through it. I take a pair of jeans and cut them too. Shoelaces and necklaces. Socks and scarfs. The birds sit at my window and watch as I tear apart my clothes to just threads and fibres. Making it manageable.

REBECCA   See you.

SAM   Was it something I said?

REBECCA   Look I don't mean to be /

SAM   / rude? It's alright. I've had worse.

REBECCA   I'm not really looking for /

SAM   / That's okay, I'm not either. Hope your day gets better.

REBECCA   Why are you talking to me?

SAM   Because it's nice to /

REBECCA   / No. Why are you talking to me?

SAM   Because you looked like you needed the company as much as me.

REBECCA   Just coffee. That's all this is. I'm not interested in /

SAM   / Just coffee.

REBECCA   Just. Coffee.

ANNA   And in amongst the scissors and the sparrows and the cuts and the crows, I made a decision. I made the decision to start my greatest task. I've made the decision to built a nest.

　　　　　A nest to protect myself, a nest to heal in, a place to rest before I'm ready to go out again. I'll build slowly, silently. Like a feather falling. I'll drink only water. I won't eat a thing. I don't want the distraction of taste. I want everything about this to be pure. After all, in order to heal you need to remove all signs of infection. I mean, that's just science… and it should be just this. Just me and this project. This wonderful project.

REBECCA   I sit staring at his flat-screen TV. I watch my own reflection back at me. Looking at it makes it hard to breathe – sometimes I get these feelings that make it hard to breathe. I called my doctor and he said I should go for a walk to try and calm down. I told him to go fuck himself.

SAM   My throat dries as I walk through the door at work. Even though I get told I'm good at my job. Even though I get told I'm a good team player. Even though – most of the time – I like what I do. Still. The simple fact is – my badge at work reads Samantha. Samantha.

REBECCA   That flat-screen is one of the few traces he ever existed. He wanted a fifty-two inch. And it wasn't to compensate for anything, he actually has quite a nice dick. He asked if he could come around tonight to pick it up. I said sure, come on over. A sledgehammer at the hardware place around the corner costs exactly £22.55.

SAM   It's two lives, two different me's. One either side of that door.

REBECCA   So long, fifty-two inches of Samsung shite. So long. And I hit it.

SAM   But not for much longer.

REBECCA   Fuck you! Circuit board, black screen, wires.

SAM   I make a promise to myself.

REBECCA   Fuck you!

SAM   Samantha won't be around for much longer.

REBECCA   And I hit it again!

ANNA   Good riddance! I throw the entire contents of my fridge out the window. And, not one person noticed.

REBECCA   Then I picture his face. My face. His face. My face. I can't do this. I can't see him.

ANNA   I've kept the tins. Seemed dangerous to throw them from so far up.

REBECCA   I can't let him see me like this. I haven't washed since Wednesday. I grab my keys, open the door

and run up the stairs, fourth floor. I've never
met her but I hear her sing though the ceiling.

Hello?

ANNA   I thought I'd at least have a few months until the
voices came.

REBECCA   Hello? I was wondering if I could come in.

ANNA   Where?

REBECCA   Into your flat. It's Rebecca from downstairs.

ANNA   Who?

REBECCA   I wondered if I could use your phone.

ANNA   Why?

REBECCA   I've locked myself out.

ANNA   What?

REBECCA   Be great just to come in for a second.

ANNA   How?

REBECCA   The key turns in the main lock. Doc Marten boots
on concrete steps. Size twelves. First floor.

ANNA   No. Sorry.

REBECCA   Second floor.

ANNA   Sorry.

REBECCA   Third floor. I sit on the ground and tuck myself
into her doorframe.

ANNA   Sorry?

REBECCA   He calls out my name as he knocks the front door
and apologises for having to use his key.

ANNA   I used to hear him shout and swear.

REBECCA   Heavy footsteps on those floorboards we spent last
summer sanding. Actually I did the sanding. It was
me who sanded those floorboards.

Fuck.

ANNA   He is shouting about a TV and shouting about
            Rebecca and I hear her twitch against my door.

REBECCA   Take the telly and leave.

ANNA   I hear him swearing and stomping. And I put my
            hand on the chain.

REBECCA   Please just let me in. He could have a hammer.

ANNA   I hear the pounding of metal on glass.

REBECCA   Just let me in.

ANNA   I hear him crash into the hall. One hand is on the
            chain. My other on the door handle.

REBECCA   Please.

ANNA   I… Sorry.

REBECCA   He shouts into the hall.

ANNA   I'm sorry.

REBECCA   He slams the door closed and throws the hammer
            against it.

ANNA   I'd like it to stop, now, please.

REBECCA   I hear him shift his weight.

ANNA   He stands just eight feet below her.

REBECCA   Please.

            Silence.

ANNA   And he begins to take the calming concrete steps
            down, closer to the ground now. Third floor.

REBECCA   Second floor.

ANNA   First floor.

REBECCA   Yale lock. Door slam.

            Silence.

ANNA   I take a tissue out of my pocket and post it through
            the letter box. She pulls it out the other side.

REBECCA	You could have just let me in.
SAM	I begin to pick the scabs on my knuckles and blood starts trickling down my fingers.
ANNA	I'm sorry I didn't.
REBECCA	Where are you going?
SAM	The red falls onto the blue of my uniform.
REBECCA	Are you there?
SAM	Someone calls me 'Samantha'.
REBECCA	She retreats into her flat.
SAM	My hand throbs.
ANNA	I haven't heard my own voice in months.
REBECCA	The TV gets switched on.
SAM	I wrap a tissue around it.
ANNA	I had forgotten what I sounded like.
SAM	Blood still rises through the paper.
ANNA	I'd forgotten I could speak.
REBECCA	The TV gets even louder. The sound of animals fighting.
ANNA	My stomach rumbles.
SAM	Samantha is gone.
REBECCA	I rest my head on her front door.
ANNA	My stomach growls.
SAM	Samantha is long gone.
REBECCA	I fucking hate nature programmes.
ANNA	The day after the door incident she posted a piece of paper through my door with the words – 'What's wrong with you?' I ripped it into twelve equal pieces and placed them in the ice-cube tray. Filled it with water and left them to freeze. I'm allowed three ice cubes a day.

SAM	You're quiet.
REBECCA	I must admit I've got a craving for something a little stronger.
SAM	I don't drink.
REBECCA	You don't drink?
SAM	Is that a bad thing?
REBECCA	I mean if someone doesn't drink... well it suggests... I don't want to... It's just. You know.
SAM	Don't worry. There isn't anything wrong.
ANNA	And just for a blink, I realise the words.
SAM	It's just.
ANNA	Heal.
SAM	When you grow up around...
ANNA	Holy.
REBECCA	It's okay. I don't need to know.
ANNA	Whole.
REBECCA	I like a drink, I hope that won't be a thing, like a... thing.
SAM	You can do what you want.
	What? What is it?
REBECCA	No it's nothing.
SAM	What is it?
ANNA	It's exhausting.
REBECCA	Well. It's just.
ANNA	Change is exhausting.
REBECCA	We still don't really... I mean.
ANNA	But I must remain pure.
REBECCA	I don't really know anything about you.

ANNA   I must remain.

SAM   You want to know something about me?

REBECCA   Sure.

SAM   This – is one of my favourite songs.

REBECCA   I don't know it.

SAM   Well you're missing out.

REBECCA   I suppose I could try something different.

SAM   Something alternative?

REBECCA   Something alternative.

SAM   Want to know something else about me?

REBECCA   What?

SAM   I really love to dance.

REBECCA   Dance? Why is it that I think you have lots of
              secrets?

SAM   Who doesn't?

              Silence.

ANNA   Minutes and hours are liquid now. It's just seasons
              and celebrations that help me notice time has
              passed. I like it when they put up the Christmas
              lights. They reflect off my window and turn the
              ceiling into a haze of red and greens. But there is
              no time for such indulgences. Not when my
              project needs to be finished. I stick to a schedule.
              My schedule that allows for washing, building,
              sleeping and dancing. Dancing is an important
              part. I was a good dancer as a child and if you
              don't use it, you lose it.

SAM   Come on, you know you want to.

REBECCA   What? Here?

SAM   Sure why not.

ANNA   It's good to make sure I can still stand.

REBECCA   It's in a coffee shop.

SAM   There is music. The lighting is low. No one will
            watch.

REBECCA   Everyone will watch.

SAM   Well then let them.

REBECCA   He hands out his hand.

ANNA   It's good to ensure all my parts still work.

SAM   Her palm slips into mine.

ANNA   I close my eyes

            I imagine someone else there.

            I imagine my big brother there.

            Holding me. Keeping me close.

            We're children again

            Safe and lost

            Smiling and laughing.

SAM   See no one noticed.

REBECCA   You're a good dancer.

ANNA   Thank you. That's what I should have said.

SAM   I need to go get ready for work.

ANNA   I should have said thank you to my brother for
            dancing with me.

SAM   I just. Saw the time.

ANNA   And I get a tear of missing him, straight through
            me.

SAM   I'll see you soon. Yeah?

ANNA   But missing someone is a distraction I don't need.
            Frankly, I should know better.

REBECCA   See you.

ANNA   I feel so faint that I can feel my pulse in my eyes.

SAM   See you.

           Silence.

ANNA   Is he your boyfriend?

REBECCA   Nah… I mean… no.

ANNA   What happened to him, the other man, the man
           who lived with you?

REBECCA   Christopher? We separated. He found someone
           else. My mother always said he had the eyes of a
           liar, I always thought they were beautiful, and now
           he is busy using them looking at his new
           girlfriend, at his brand-new life…

ANNA   Did he hit you?

REBECCA   She stands close to the door now. I've never seen
           her face. When I look through the letter box I see
           her ribcage. I think she might be naked, but her
           flat is dark and it's hard to tell.

ANNA   What did you do with the bits of the TV you
           smashed up? Could I have them?

REBECCA   I threw them out… sorry.

ANNA   Why do you come up?

REBECCA   Because I might be able to help.

ANNA   I don't need help.

REBECCA   You need to leave your flat at some point.

ANNA   I'm not going to talk to you if you don't stop this.

REBECCA   But I could help you.

ANNA   No you can't.

REBECCA   Let me help you.

ANNA   I'm going now.

REBECCA   No. Please.

ANNA   Bye.

REBECCA   Please... Anna? Anna? Are you still there?

            Please don't...

            Leave.

            Silence.

ANNA   What happened to all your friends? You used to
            have your parties? I could hear them through the
            floorboards.

REBECCA   The thing is – They were Christopher's friends.

ANNA   You don't need them.

REBECCA   You think?

ANNA   There is only one way to find out.

SAM   You were a good dancer.

REBECCA   No one ever told me that before.

SAM   Then you've been dancing with the wrong people.

REBECCA   You're telling me.

SAM   You should go out dancing more.

REBECCA   I'm too old for all that.

SAM   Never too old to dance. Maybe I'll take you
            dancing? Proper dancing.

REBECCA   Maybe.

SAM   Go on.

REBECCA   I don't... I don't think so. I'm not really... Sorry.

SAM   Oh, fucksake.

ANNA   It's hammers and hard work and drills and dust.
            I take out all the light bulbs. I use knives to peel
            off the wallpaper. I unscrew all the cupboard
            doors. Removing all the corners where anything
            could hide.

REBECCA   I'd be too nervous to dance properly, in front of you. Especially if you're sober. How can I impress you with my moves?

SAM   You want to impress me?

REBECCA   No. Yes. I don't know.

SAM   If you /

REBECCA   / I don't know. I don't know if I want to impress you or not.

SAM   It's alright /

REBECCA   / You just can't… You can't just. You've no idea.

ANNA   My flat is being taken back to its bare bones. Its skeleton.

REBECCA   I've got things to work out… and I just think /

SAM   / yeah well who doesn't have things to work out.

REBECCA   Everyone else?

SAM   That's not true.

REBECCA   Well that's what it feels like.

SAM   You want me to walk you home?

ANNA   They've been good to me. Those birds. People have never given birds enough credit. They squawk and shout as I begin to tear up the floorboards. Heaving them up. Pulling them out. It's going to be hard to dance when the floorboards are not there – I know… but… but… but sometimes, just sometimes, you need to… do… I hope I haven't… focus. Anna. Bloody focus.

REBECCA   Do you want to come in?

SAM   I need to watch the time, I'm /

REBECCA   / you really hate being late, don't you?

ANNA   To be reinvented as a bird.

SAM   This is a nice building, I bet you've nice neighbours.

REBECCA	That's a long story.
ANNA	To take flight.
REBECCA	There is this girl, above me, I think she's got some... I mean...
ANNA	Those brilliant birds, what I wouldn't give to /
SAM	/ Hello? Anna?
	Anyone in?
REBECCA	You know you don't have to do this. I know you're off-duty.
SAM	I offered.
REBECCA	She never leaves.
SAM	Are you sure?
REBECCA	I promise.
ANNA	I just want them to leave.
REBECCA	Anna? You there? I brought someone who might be able to help.
ANNA	I just want them to stay.
SAM	Keep an eye on her.
REBECCA	But what if she... does something.
SAM	There is only so much you can do for people. I don't usually do home visits.
ANNA	It's been a long time since I've heard people talk to each other.
REBECCA	You don't have any magic words?
SAM	None of the words I know are magic.
REBECCA	It's all a bit fucked. Isn't it?
SAM	Maybe.
REBECCA	Maybe not?
	Silence.

ANNA   And they kiss. I can hear it. Their lips connecting.

REBECCA   I thought you were running late?

SAM   I can be a few minutes late.

REBECCA   Good.

ANNA   They kiss again.

REBECCA   I take his hands and I place them on my sides.

SAM   Tender. So fucking tender.

ANNA   I can hear them breathe.

REBECCA   I slip my hands down his sides.

SAM   Deep and hard.

REBECCA   I want him. His palms. His lips.

ANNA   I can hear the tug of hands on clothes.

SAM   And it's just this moment

REBECCA   Here

SAM   Now

ANNA   Maybe I want to be kissed.

REBECCA   His hand slips onto my hip bone.

SAM   Her bare skin.

ANNA   Maybe I want to be touched.

SAM   Under her belt, under the jeans.

ANNA   I want to be touched.

REBECCA   I can feel his fingers.

ANNA   I want to be there

REBECCA   Up against the door

SAM   I carry her weight

ANNA   I just want

SAM   I love it.

REBECCA   Don't stop.

ANNA   Please stop.

SAM   I love it.

REBECCA   Don't stop.

ANNA   Please stop.

SAM   I love it.

REBECCA   Don't stop.

ANNA   Stop.

REBECCA   Fuck.

SAM   Fuck.

ANNA   Stop.

REBECCA   Fuck.

SAM   Fuck.

ANNA   Fucking leave me alone!

Silence.

SAM   What was that?

REBECCA   Nothing. It's nothing.

SAM   She pulls my hand out of her jeans.

REBECCA   You've beautiful eyes.

SAM   Puts my fingers in her mouth. Fuck.

REBECCA   Do you really have to go to work?

Pity.

ANNA   My eyes gaze at the door. Looking at the letter box. Eyes wet. Hands numb. The nature channel on in the background. The sound of wolves howling fills my flat. I don't miss it. And it's not a lie... just a past-tense truth. I really should get back to my nest.

REBECCA   It's the way he looks at me, you know?

SAM   I think of my fingers in her mouth. I'm thinking of
             that way she... Been a long time since... It had
             just been a long time.

REBECCA   I mean I'm just pretty sure my vagina is an idiot.

SAM   Daydreaming of dancing, wandering my way to
             work and I hear this laughter.

REBECCA   He isn't like anyone I've ever met.

SAM   A tag team of teenagers talking tits, teams and
             Tennent's. It's headphones in and hands in
             pockets. I turn a corner and I can still hear their
             hollers. Swaggering along in my shadow. One of
             them mutters the word faggot. I shake it off. One
             of them brushes against my jacket. I shake it off.
             One of them pushes me. So I turn and I look at
             them – and I'm faced with a dozen eyes, lit with
             the surprise at the sound of my voice saying –

             What do you want from me?
             I said – what the fuck do you want from me? Or
             are you done?
             Are you done having a long, hard, look?

             Good. So fucking move along and leave me alone.

             Silence.

             A flash in front of my eyes. A fist. And I'm down.
             My face in the dirt of a puddle. My cheek burns –
             I see feet – I'm surrounded.

             I pick myself up – a kick to my back, down again,
             I pick myself up – a shoe to my shin, to my wrist,
             to my spine, down again, a trainer slams on my
             hand, I try to pick myself up – A foot to my face.
             Blood fills my nose, blood fills my mouth.

             Their laughs in the air, I claw the ground – I can't
             breathe, I try to pick myself up – they grab my
             jacket and push me to the pavement, down again,
             dirt in my eyes, blood in my throat, I try to – they
             kick – down again, I try to – their fists – down
             again, I try to – down again and again and again, I
             open my eyes to the flash of a boot and /

REBECCA   / You're quiet.

SAM   I hear them spit. It lands on my cheek

ANNA   I'm just…

SAM   Blood just trickles… out my ear.

ANNA   Tired.

SAM   Eyes just… mouth just… pulse just… stop.

REBECCA   You've been busy?

ANNA   Yeah. Yeah I've been really busy.

REBECCA   Good to keep busy.

           I was thinking. About how useful it can be to talk.
           And I just wanted to say, if you want to talk about
           what's happening with you. I can listen. If you
           want someone to listen I will listen. I'm a good
           listener. Everyone said so… and I heard that, cos
           I'm a good listener. That was a joke.

ANNA   Tired. Rebecca. I'm too tired for this.

REBECCA   I think it's okay to tell people things.

ANNA   I'm not so sure.

REBECCA   I think it's okay to share what happened to you…
           if anything at all happened…

ANNA   You want to know what happened to me?

REBECCA   Yeah. Of course I do.

ANNA   You really want to know?

REBECCA   Yes!

ANNA   You know the twin towers?
           I was there. 9/11.
           You know those London bombings? I was
           there too.

           Lockerbie. I saw the plane fall from the sky.
           Chernobyl. I watched the trees melt. The truth is I
           was forced to dig the graves for Auschwitz.

I also have cancer and HIV and bird flu. I've burned books and bodies. I've recruited child soldiers. I've stoned women to death. I injected heroin into pregnant mothers and I've evicted people on their birthdays. I've also placed pillows over the faces of newborns, set homeless people on fire, starved families and withheld drinking water, buried people alive and left them to rot and I've plunged puppies into boiling water.

I've hung people from hooks and watched them bleed to death. I heard them cry. I heard them shout. I heard them plead for their lives and still I helped build the first nuclear bomb. I set it off.

I mean I gave Pocahontas smallpox.
I gave Myra Hindley that haircut and I told her she looked nice.
I rejected Hitler from art school.
And, I drowned the last dodo.

That's what happened to me.

REBECCA   Anna?

ANNA   Yes.

REBECCA   I'm not sure that's actually what happened.

ANNA   I can promise you, that's what did happen.

REBECCA   Can I call someone for you? Your brother? He used to visit?

ANNA   I should go.

REBECCA   Don't.

ANNA   I've got things to do.

REBECCA   I lie in bed and I hear Anna, upstairs. Moving around and she cries. Occasionally I hear her crying but who doesn't cry… occasionally. I check my phone – no new messages. And it's starting to keep me up at night. It's starting to make me. Because I'm not good with… When I think someone might be… the thing is… even when I was a child… Christopher. Fuck. His side of the bed is... fuck. Because he was meant to be... and we were meant to be... I mean what am I... How the hell am I meant to...

SAM   I've had an accident.

REBECCA   My phone shakes and shivers.

SAM   Sorry I didn't text.

REBECCA   Are you being dramatic? Send.

SAM   Sixteen stitches.

ANNA   My eyes get fuzzy these days.

SAM   Bruised rib.

ANNA   My hair is starting to come out.

SAM   Three missing teeth, two black eyes, a broken wrist.

ANNA   My limbs ache.

SAM   I'm lucky it's not worse. Discharged this morning.

REBECCA   Do you want me to bring grapes?

ANNA   I hear this tapping.

SAM   Honestly, I'm not ready for company.

ANNA   Outside my window is a creature, a skeleton-looking creature, its beak tapping on the window.

REBECCA   Don't you like grapes?

ANNA   It's dirty-looking, covered in oil.

REBECCA   Shall we meet for coffee?

ANNA   He has an eye missing and barbed wire around his feet.

REBECCA   Sam? I'd like to see you.

ANNA   And as I get closer, I realise it's a pelican. And I don't know much about pelicans but I know they aren't supposed to look like that. So I open the window and he doesn't move. He just looks at me, through his one eye.

SAM   I look a bit different don't I.

REBECCA   Sore. It looks, really, really, sore. Can I hug you?

ANNA   I put my arms around the pelican and pick him off the windowsill. He is as light as air.

SAM   They said I'm lucky I didn't puncture a lung.

REBECCA   Do you want me to call your family?

SAM   They wouldn't… they aren't really… but thanks.

ANNA   I put him in my nest. And he just looks at me through that one eye.

SAM   This is sore enough – I can't imagine being in a car crash like you.

ANNA   I carefully untangle the barbed wire from around his feet.

REBECCA   I wasn't in a car crash.

SAM   What do you mean?

REBECCA   My face? It was an accident. At first. Then I made it worse.

SAM   I think you're beautiful.

REBECCA   I should have been… honest.

ANNA   He is barely alive but he is alive.

REBECCA   You've been really… you know.

ANNA   I get a wet wipe and run it along his back. The fabric turns black with oil.

SAM   Honest.

REBECCA   What is it?

ANNA   The oil is coming off slowly.

SAM   The accident… incident. Well. It made some things very clear to me. It made me realise that you're really special to me and I want to be… honest. With you.

REBECCA   What are you talking about?

SAM   I haven't always... been like – I haven't always...
            I should have planned this... fuck. It's just, I
            wasn't... I'm not... Technically. I was born. With
            a woman's body.

ANNA   And suddenly the pelican shakes his head and
            makes this deafening sound.

SAM   Please understand.

ANNA   He cries out, half in pain and half in joy and falls
            into my hands.

REBECCA   I let you kiss me... and I'm not...

SAM   Let me explain.

ANNA   And I continue to wipe the oil and the blood and
            the salt and the grit and the petrol and the fumes
            and the glass out of the bird's feathers.

REBECCA   I slip away.

ANNA   This could take me a lifetime.

REBECCA   Delete it all. Delete everything.

ANNA   The pelican sleeps in my nest and I lie next to
            him, with a piece of broken mirror up to his
            mouth, making sure he is still breathing.

REBECCA   I drink mouthfuls of Merlot and I smoke cheap
            cigarettes. Amount of fucks given? Zero.

SAM   I go to the doctor's and ask to speak to someone.
            I tell them. I tell them about every wound, every
            worry.

ANNA   He is getting paler. The pelican. He is getting
            worse, and this nest is getting neglected. My nest
            is far from complete.

SAM   They ask me questions. They talk trauma and
            childhood and change.

REBECCA   I would have thought I'd have learnt by now, how
            not to fuck it up quite so fantastically.

ANNA   And even I know he's got to eat something.

SAM   No more hiding.

REBECCA   My phone bursts with beeps.

SAM   Sam misses you.

REBECCA   Don't talk about yourself in the third person it
            makes you sound like a dick.

ANNA   I get a tin of beans. One that my brother left. Open
            it. Take a spoon. Offer a single bean to the pelican.
            I mean I don't know what pelicans eat.

            Go on then.

            Eat it.

            And he just looks at me, with that one pale eye.
            Flutters his feathers and shakes his head. I mean,
            I'm pretty sure he shakes his head.

SAM   I didn't mean to hurt you. I'm sorry.

REBECCA   Delete my number.

ANNA   Eat.

SAM   I'm sorry.

REBECCA   Delete my number.

ANNA   Eat.

SAM   I'm sorry.

REBECCA   Delete my number.

ANNA   Eat.

SAM   I'm sorry.

REBECCA   Enough now or I'll call the police.

ANNA   If he doesn't eat. He'll die here.

SAM   And just like that.

ANNA   I don't want you to die.

            Not like this.

            Not slowly like this.

SAM	Fuck her.
REBECCA	I can't remember how this goes any more.
ANNA	And I place that bean in my mouth.
	And I swallow.
REBECCA	I forget what forwards feels like.
ANNA	See, it's not so bad. The pelican just looks at me.
REBECCA	A life so empty it echoes.
ANNA	Go on then. I'll show you, again.

ANNA's long speech:

And I take another bean, on that spoon, and I put it in my mouth. I haven't eaten solids in weeks. You should be honoured. And with that, the pelican looks at me and opens his beak. I take a spoon of beans and drop it into his mouth. He swallows. And another, and another, and another.

Barely alive but we are alive.

REBECCA	Volume. Eleven.
SAM	Come on then.
ANNA	He looks at me, with thanks.
SAM	I stand in front of that mirror.
REBECCA	Place the CD in the machine.
ANNA	It's different now the pelican is here. It's different not being alone.
SAM	Practising. Practising standing.
ANNA	You better get better – you hear me?
SAM	Practise catching my breath.
REBECCA	Who knew that sherry and vodka and tequila went so well together.
ANNA	This is no time to give up on me.
SAM	Practising. Practising moving.
ANNA	Whatever happens, we go through this together.

REBECCA   If I'm going to fall apart. I might as well do it
           loudly.

SAM   Practising being me.

           And I put my fist through the wall. Here. Now.
           Everything changes. Because it has to. It has to. It
           has to. It has to. It has to. It has to. It has to. It has
           to. It has to. Change. It's just got to.

REBECCA   When was the last time you had sex?

ANNA   I could smell the red wine through the letter box.

REBECCA   I've been drinking but I am not drunk. Why don't
           you go out any more?

ANNA   Why don't you?

REBECCA   What happened to your brother? He used to visit.

ANNA   He pays my rent. He is embarrassed of me.

REBECCA   Do you want to come down to mine?

ANNA   I turn and look at the pelican in my nest, our nest.

SAM   And this is the last time.

REBECCA   I'd like to help you.

SAM   I make a promise to myself.

ANNA   Stop trying.

SAM   This is the last time I'll start again.

ANNA   I said – stop trying.

           Silence.

REBECCA   What happened to you Anna? What was so bad
           that being in there is better than being out here?
           Did someone do something to you? Did someone
           do something terrible... Or did you do something
           terrible?

           Silence.

ANNA   It's just... The whole thing is... I missed my bus.

REBECCA   That's it?

ANNA   One day, I missed my bus into town and came back to my flat and I haven't been out since... because that was the final thing, it was the final thing I could let go wrong.

REBECCA   She looks through the letter box for the first time

ANNA   It was just. Lots of things. Lots of small things.

Like ants. Like ants who slowly pick apart what's left of the animal. I had to close the door before they tore everything. I had to close the door to save... I've never been fond of insects. It's the one type of nature programme I can't watch.

REBECCA   Her eyes are bloodshot and hollow and her skin is a strange tinge of yellow and blue.

ANNA   She has a scar on her cheek and red wine on her lips.

Stillness and silence.

REBECCA   I saw Christopher in the street last week. I hid from him. I just hid. He'd been shopping in Mothercare and he hates shopping. But there he was with a teddy tucked under his... and his girlfriend with this big... That was supposed to have been me.

ANNA   You could still be a /

REBECCA   / Don't. Don't say things like that.

Silence.

I don't know how I didn't see it all.

I suppose I just saw what I wanted to see.

ANNA   The pelican winks at me with his one eye.

REBECCA   Do you think I'm having a breakdown?

ANNA   Maybe.

REBECCA   What should I do?

ANNA   I'm not sure I'm the best person to ask.

            Silence.

REBECCA   I think this is what loneliness is, isn't it? I
            always wondered what it felt like and I think it
            feels like this.

ANNA   What does it feel like?

REBECCA   It feels… surprisingly boring… and painful… and
            normal… and dark.

ANNA   Well they say the darkest moment is right before
            the dawn, before the light.

REBECCA   Then where is the light?

            Silence.

SAM   Sweat trickles down my neck.

            I pass a group of teenagers on the street. My
            muscles tense and I hold my breath.

ANNA   Me and the pelican allow ourselves four beans on
            the spoon, and each can is approximately twenty
            spoonfuls which makes it ten spoonfuls each. The
            beans are greasy and shine in the silver of the
            spoon, but I am choosing not to mind.

SAM   I get scared sometimes. Sometimes I just get.

            But I must refuse.

            I work really hard at refusing to stop. These streets
            are mine. This is my city. I can still breathe. I can
            still blink.

REBECCA   Work tomorrow. I set out my clothes. I make my
            packed lunch. I set my alarm. I bought a deep dark
            foundation to cover my scar. I'd rather people
            thought I fake-tanned than ate glass.

ANNA   The pelican sits and watches me finish my nest.
            He spends his day watching the Discovery
            Channel. We both like programmes about places
            we will never go.

REBECCA   I feel the groove on my cheek.

                The line of a scar.

ANNA   The trouble is. We had our last can of beans three days ago and his sparkle is fading again. His feathers are beginning to fall out.

                And even I know he can't go hungry again.

REBECCA   I tell myself. I can do this.

ANNA   I won't let things fall apart again

REBECCA   I tell myself. I can do this.

ANNA   I won't let something else fail.

REBECCA   I can do this.

ANNA   But I can't go the shop... not even for him.

SAM   That person in the reflection is older than he was. I look a bit like my grandfather. And that makes me... I don't know. It just makes me. Relieved. No syringes. No surgery. No stitches. Just this. Sam. He was always there.

REBECCA   I think of some stories to tell.

                I practise my smile in the mirror.

ANNA   And then I see it... I see...

REBECCA   I pause and practise.

ANNA   There is no ground left to stand on, all the floorboards are gone.

REBECCA   Smile. No smile.

ANNA   There is nothing left to take apart. And I haven't found any more sense. This isn't a purpose. This isn't pure.

REBECCA   No smile. Smile. I see it now. It's hard. It's hard to see the other side of it all and come back.

ANNA   This project, which I have poured myself out into... it's... not going... this isn't... it's not what

I had… this isn't what I… it's… I'm… I still
feel… I still…

Silence.

SAM   Anna? Is that Anna?

ANNA   This voice through the buzzer.

SAM   It's Sam. I'm Rebecca's… friend. Can you let
           me in?

ANNA   Why do you want to see her?

SAM   I want to post something through her door.

ANNA   But she isn't in.

SAM   It's just a note. Only a note.

ANNA   Just slip it through the front door. She'll get it
           there. What is it?

SAM   My new number. I got a new phone, a new
           number. It's just in case she wants to get in
           touch… I'm just trying to reconnect with a few
           folk. Anyway make sure she gets it – yeah?

ANNA   Sam?

SAM   Yeah.

ANNA   What's it like?

SAM   What's what like?

           Silence.

ANNA   What's it like out there?

           Silence.

SAM   Well it's cold. They think it might rain soon.

           You alright? You okay?

           Silence.

ANNA   I'm fine. I've got things to do. Things that need
           doing.

SAM	What are you doing?
ANNA	I don't know.

Silence.

| SAM | I know that you're scared. |

Silence.

I am too.

Silence.

But it won't be that wet. Honest. Nothing that won't pass. Good weather for ducks – my dad used to say that. Good weather for ducks.

Silence.

Look I need to get my bus back. I'm only on my lunch break.

I'm sorry Anna.

Silence.

ANNA	Good luck.
SAM	Good luck to you too.
ANNA	Pelican looks at me through his one eye.

I have nothing to offer you.

No one ever told me.

No one ever said how hard this was all going to be.

Silence.

| REBECCA | I come home to a note with eleven digits on it. |

Guilt. As I pin that note to the door of my fridge and picture his face.

I stare at it as my hand runs along my scar.

| ANNA | Me and the pelican lie down in the nest together. |

His eye begins to roll back into his head.

SAM   My phone lights up with life.

REBECCA   I'm embarrassed about how I behaved.

ANNA   Maybe some silence would be a good thing.

REBECCA   I'd like to see you – if you'd like to see me?

ANNA   I run my hand along the pelican's beak. The cold makes our breath cloud in the air and I wrap myself inside his wings. His feathers brush onto my back and his warmth washes over me. He is terribly gentle for such a big ungainly bird. A true credit to his species.

But now, just a little rest, dear pelican. Just a little… silence, for once, a little sleep. We'll be up again in no time and we best be rested for all the things we need to do.

Did you hear me? Pelican. Just a little… We'll close our eyes… Only for a minute.

Only for a…

SAM   I'm sorry.

REBECCA   He drops his cigarette to the ground.

SAM   I wanted to say it in person.

REBECCA   Handsome. I find him handsome.

SAM   I didn't mean to hurt. It was unexpected. I wasn't expecting you.

REBECCA   I am not exactly who I expected either.

SAM   Is that a good thing?

REBECCA   I don't know.

So what… are you… you live as a… I mean I don't want to be… but is it just /

SAM   / I just live as me.

REBECCA   But you're /

SAM	/ I'm just me. That's all.
	I changed jobs. Been doing some online dating. Nothing serious though, everyone seems so... boring.
REBECCA	I'm doing better, too.
SAM	I'm glad.
REBECCA	Me too.
ANNA	The pelican wakes me when his wing slips off my skin. I pick up that piece of mirror to check pelican's breath and I see myself in it. I see... this person. This... woman. I'd forgotten, I'd forgotten what she looked like. When did she get so tired? When did I... With that I cut the tip of my finger on the mirror. A droplet of blood to the surface. Blood. Pumping blood.
	Barely alive but we are alive.
SAM	It's freezing – do you want to go inside.
REBECCA	No... I... I don't have time, not today.
SAM	Forecast says it's going to rain.
REBECCA	I don't believe in forecasts.
ANNA	I clutch that shard of mirror. Blood trickles down my finger.
	I exist. I exist.
REBECCA	I was horrible to you. I said awful things /
SAM	/ I forgive you. For those things you said. How you behaved. I forgive you.
ANNA	I look at the pelican. Search in the corners of my nest, find £1.56, wrap scraps of fabric around myself. Put my hand on the chain latched across the door, and I pull it across.
	I open the door.
REBECCA	You know you didn't have to lie.

SAM   Of course I did.

ANNA   It's one foot, then the other. Third floor. Second.
            First. Ground floor. Front door.

REBECCA   You don't know what I would have /

SAM   / Yes I do.

ANNA   It's been nearly two Christmases since I was an
            ant on the ground instead of a bird in the sky.
            Look at it. Look at it all, out there.

REBECCA   But I /

SAM   / Look. I wasn't lying when I said I cared for you,
            when I said you were important. None of that was
            lies. You… well you… I've been by myself for a
            really long time. And it felt nice, it felt nice having
            someone, having you there, there in my life. I
            should have said that. That day. I should have said
            you were important to me. I've never been good at
            telling people they're important. I'm very good at
            pushing people away. I'm good at being alone.
            But here I am, with you, telling you – you're
            important to me. And it's okay, I understand if you
            can't… or won't… or whatever. But I'm here, I'm
            not running away, I'm here.

ANNA   Things look different down here. Dirtier. Messier.

            I step out the front door and just as I do /

SAM   / Snow?

REBECCA   Talk about global warming.

SAM   Looks like the forecast was wrong.

REBECCA   At least it's not raining.

ANNA   I stare at that phone box across the road and step
            into the sound of people talking and traffic, my
            eardrums burn. The snow in my eyes makes it
            look like I might be weeping. I mean I might be
            weeping.

SAM   I'm glad I met you.

REBECCA   Were you not going to come?

SAM   No. I'm just, glad I met you.

ANNA   My skin blisters with the cold. Goosebumps rise on my arms. I'd forgotten how much everything. How everything. How it. How it just. That snow.

That... snow.

REBECCA   I have to go back to work now. I'm on my lunch hour.

SAM   Quick lunch hour.

REBECCA   Yeah well, it's a lot isn't it.

It's a lot to be with someone who knows all your secrets.

SAM   Okay.

REBECCA   Okay.

ANNA   Okay.

REBECCA   If you wanted to, in time, I'd be up for a coffee.

SAM   I'd like that.

Stay warm.

REBECCA   I will.

See you around.

SAM   See you around.

ANNA   I drop those coins in the machine.

The sound of a phone ringing.

Rings again.

Please pick up.

Rings again.

Please pick up.

Rings again.

Just pick up the phone.

Rings again.

Please.

Rings again.

Please.

Rings again.

Hi, it's me... it's... yeah... it's your voice.

Gosh.

...Can you bring me some...

...I just... your voice.

...Can you...

...You...

Yes.

Thank you. Thank...

She hangs up the phone.

You.

Silence.

Gosh.

Gosh.

Silence.

My brother's voice... it rings... just here... in my...

Silence.

And I see the pelican at the window.

I quickly run up to my flat. Slam my door behind me.

The pelican looks at me, and winks with his one eye. Don't worry. My brother will arrive soon with carrier bags full of tins of beans and a smile. I will invite him for a walk in the park so that we can feed the ducks. And he'll cry into his scarf and he'll say – I'm crying tears of happiness. Even if he isn't he'll say I'm crying tears of happiness. And I'll put my arm around him and tell him, I'll tell him – everything is going to be okay.

And with that the pelican begins to flap his wings.

The pelican's cry fills my room as he jumps into the air. And then flies straight through the window. Glass. Wood. Everywhere.

REBECCA   I look up to the check the bus times.

ANNA   But you can't!

SAM   I place my headphones in my ears.

ANNA   You can't!

REBECCA   And there is something in the sky.

ANNA   But you can't!

SAM   What the hell is that?

ANNA   You... you're flying.

REBECCA   Through the snow it looks like a seagull.

ANNA   He's wobbly and he's shaking but he's... flying.

SAM   It's a...

ANNA   So long...

ALL   / Pelican.

SAM   But we are miles from the sea.

ANNA   He chose life.

SAM   He has got a long journey home.

REBECCA   Strange. I don't think I've ever seen a pelican.

SAM   I hope he makes it.

REBECCA   I suppose you'll never know what you'll see.

ANNA   We chose life.

Silence.

SAM   Pause

REBECCA   Just for a second.

ANNA   Stillness.

SAM   Just for a second.

ANNA   Pause

REBECCA   Just for a second.

ANNA   Stillness.

SAM   Just for a second.

REBECCA   Pause.

              Stillness and silence.

ANNA   I turn to my window. The one the pelican flew out
              of and it's intact.

              I press my hands on the glass and the cold reaches
              my palms, I pull away. I leave two smudges of ten
              digits. And in that moment I realise how little I
              understand.

REBECCA   The snow settles on the top of the bus stop. I put
              my phone up to my face and it's me and that little
              black lens. I turn on that camera. My mascara's
              ruined and my face glows with cold and I see the
              exact thing that is there. And it's me. All of me.
              And just as the old woman next to me lights up a
              cigarette, the bus appears. She swears and sighs
              and I take my phone and begin to call my gran.
              And a tear creeps into my eye when she says – *so
              tell me, tell me how you are.*

ANNA   My nest. My nest of floorboards and fabric and
              forks. I'll take it apart. Slowly. Like a feather
              falling. I'll put everything back into its right place.
              No, I'll find a different place for everything. No
              nest, not any more. Not flying, not yet. Just
              perched, ready for the change.

SAM   I dash under the awning of the café and put a fag
              in my mouth. It's damp, my matchbox drips with

melted snow but still, in spite of everything – the match lights. If you swallow the smoke enough, you learn to enjoy it. I'll give up eventually but for now I think I've given up enough things. Back in the world now.

Reconnect.

Still blinking. Still breathing. Still blinking. Still.

The End.

A Nick Hern Book

Swallow first published as a paperback original in Great Britain in 2015
by Nick Hern Books Limited, The Glasshouse, 49a Goldhawk Road, London
W12 8QP, in association with the Traverse Theatre, Edinburgh

Swallow copyright © 2015 Stef Smith

Stef Smith has asserted her right to be identified as the author of this work

Cover image used under licence from Shutterstock.com

Designed and typeset by Nick Hern Books, London
Printed and bound in Great Britain by CPI Group (UK) Ltd

A CIP catalogue record for this book is available from the British Library

ISBN 978 1 84842 506 4